Marketing Hacks
57 Do-It-Yourself Tactics
To Find Qualified Customers
And Make More Sales!

by Thomas J. Forgione

LEGAL DISCLAIMER

Copyright © 2015 Thomas J. Forgione

All rights reserved.

ISBN-13: 978-0692390818

ISBN-10: 0692390812

Published by: Three Twenty Publishing

1415 Hooper Avenue, Suite 302

Toms River, NJ 08753

Dedication

This book is dedicated to my wife, Francine. If it was not for her, I would not have started in this business so many years ago. She always believed in me, and although sometimes I can be hardheaded, she never gave up on me. I love you, Francine.

It is also dedicated to my family, friends, clients and students, way too many people to mention, including Glenn Foster, Art Director Extraordinaire. Glenn's beautiful graphic design always stands apart from the rest. And to Stewart Tenner, a mentor and marketing genius, who has helped me in countless ways. I appreciate your friendship and business.

A special thank you to Harlan Coben and Dr. Ian Smith who are both brilliant authors. Working with them inspired me to get this book done.

CONTENTS

CHAPTER 6

Website Design   28

CHAPTER 1

What, Another Marketing Book?

Before I explain, I want to thank you for buying my book. I know there are many books on marketing and I appreciate you choosing mine. It is an honor, and I wholeheartedly appreciate it. I hope this helps you with your marketing, and I value your opinion, so please contact me through my website at www.thomasforgione.com.

Why did I write a marketing book when there are many currently being sold? That's a great question. Well, I never considered myself a writer but after working with clients and teaching students for almost twenty years, one of the questions they posed to me over and over was, "Why don't you write a book?" So after careful consideration and deep reflection to ensure I could write a book that contained valuable information, I decided to do it. The strategies in this book are real-world strategies.

If you find any spelling or grammar mistakes or are confused by anything, you can contact me directly on my website at www.thomasforgione.com.

Thanks again!

CHAPTER 2

The Three Reasons Why You Should Listen To Me: Experience. Experience. Experience.

I was born in Newark, New Jersey, and raised by a single mother, grandmother, and grandfather in East Orange, New Jersey. My grandfather owned Orange Mattress Company with his brother, Frank, a mattress manufacturer since 1902, a family business. From the time I could talk, my mother would bring me to "The Factory," where I learned sales, marketing, and business while watching the salespeople sell, and my mother and Uncle Frank create the ads that were placed in newspapers and magazines. It was the best education someone in my field could get.

My mother married my father, Phil, who was in the bar business. And when I was old enough, I bounced around from the bar business to the mattress business. (No pun intended.) In the bar business you really learn about human behavior, which also helps in marketing. You learn empathy and how to respond to every situation, which also helps in sales. Many lessons I learned from the bar business I hope you never have to deal with. That is for another book.

I have always been extroverted and loved music, so I gravitated toward the nightclub business and became a DJ, which I enjoyed for many years. Later I had some minor success as a union actor, which was when I met my wife, Francine, also an actor.

After acting, I started in professional sales and sales management, a profession where I was successful. I managed the sales and marketing of a merchant services company and increased their company sales to a point where they were offered a buyout from their competitor that they could not refuse.

After a few years in sales, this new crazy thing called the Internet was all over the news. It seemed like the Wild West to me (and it was), so I looked for a way to make some money with this Internet thing. I started developing websites in 1995, and after a year or two, I was contracted to develop the websites for the company who manufactured electronic toys such as Barbie®, Playskool®, Fisher-Price®, Hot Wheels® and home electronics such as Timex®, Zenith®, and Soundesign® to name a few.

Then things really started to happen. My sales team was selling websites and related services, when clients started asking for other stuff: Internet marketing, search engine optimization, ads, brochures, direct mail, and so forth. So we then expanded to become a non-commission marketing and advertising agency.

In 1998 I became an instructor at a local college, where I taught classes in Advertising and Marketing, How to Start a Business, Webmaster Certificate, Search Engine Optimization, HTML, Website Design and Marketing, and Web Server Administration, to name a few.

Why the Long Bio?

As I say in my seminars and classes, it is important that you know I am not a theory-based marketing "guru." The tactics I present in this book are from over twenty years' experience working with clients in the marketing field, and forty-five years of experience in wholesale and retail business within multiple industries. This book will give you frank instruction without the fluff and baloney you might be getting now from other consultants.

To sign up for free marketing information, or to contact me, visit my website at www.thomasforgione.com

CHAPTER 3

There Are No Quick Tricks In Real Marketing

People ask me, "What are some quick tricks for marketing my business?" They are looking for quick fixes, techniques, or something new that will propel their business forward at lightning speeds.

They are looking for advertising that will work with one placement and little frequency, or a website that will bring them thousands of customers without any effort.

There is nothing wrong to look for tricks and techniques to help you advance your business; however, I find that the effort wasted looking for them would have been better spent seeking methods that others have had success with.

Many business owners look at a publication or website and see their competition advertising and think, "Oh no! My competition has a jump on me! What am I to do? I know, I will advertise my business there, too. I'll show them." The better thing to do would be to take a deep breath. Research the medium to see if it is where your customers are and then track to see if your competitor is still there after a while. Or if it is someone in a similar industry but not a competitor, why not call and ask if it is working for them before taking the plunge?

When you see your competition trying things once and then never again, it almost always indicates that it did not work. Or the money ran out. Or they tried it for one shot to get the coupon book or coupon mailer or newspaper salesperson off their back. They did not realize that certain techniques must be used in an advertisement in order for it to be effective. I am not saying that there are not new and tested mediums out there to advertise your business in; there are. But don't just jump in without knowing if your market (customer base) is served there. Make sure your customers, by matching their demographics to the medium, are looking or listening where you are advertising. This is an easy and much-needed step that many business owners do not get right.

As a business owner it is your job to show your customers, and your competition, that you are in it for the long haul. By ensuring that your advertising and marketing are presented in the right places, your customers will feel you know them better. Someone who sells to me who really knows what I do and what I need always gets the sale over someone who does not.

But in case you're still looking for that quick trick, I will give you a great technique I have found to be the most successful marketing and advertising technique known to man and womankind.

Are you ready for it?

Here it is.

Stop looking for tricks and start advertising and marketing your business the right way! Get to it! What are you waiting for?!

To sign up for free marketing information, or to contact me, visit my website at www.thomasforgione.com

CHAPTER 4

Why Is Marketing Important?

So, why marketing? Why should you constantly market your business? Why is it important? For most businesses, the main goal, is to make money. You must market your business to attract a steady stream of new customers. In addition to gaining new customers you also use marketing to keep your existing customers buying from you, and buying from you more often.

Marketing is everything; communicating with your customers on a website, through social media, through webinars, e-mail, newsletters, TV commercials, and so forth. It's all about communicating your message to the right prospects, who in turn will become your customers. Now, of course, the message to your existing customers will be different because they already are your customers. So you might not have to sell them on you as often, but you still have to refresh their memory as to why they did business with you in the first place and how great you are. And you keep in touch with your customers through marketing.

Did you ever have an idea, and about a month later you see somebody else implementing the idea? It was a great idea, and you know that person is making money from doing it. The only thing that stopped you from doing it yourself was fear or the I-don't-have-the-time syndrome. Well, that happens all the time, especially in marketing. You have a great marketing idea. You want to implement it, and then you don't. And then you see your competition doing it. Well, that's a problem. You need to go out there and be first, especially if you have a better company or product.

The biggest obstacle that I see in businesses is not the lack of ideas, it's implementation. Lack of implementation is a common disease. And the only way to cure it is to do it, keep doing it, keep tweaking it, and keep moving forward. If you want more, you've got to do more. If you do more, you'll get more. And when you get more, you have the time to do more.

Whatever tactics you decide to use in your overall marketing strategy, you must never do only one thing at a time. One thing at a time is very slow and painful. You want to do five or ten things at a time to try to get new customers. You want to put together a strategic marketing plan that is designed to make your existing customers buy from you, buy more from you, buy more often from you, and refer. That's seems easier said than done. However, it's doable. Successful companies do it, and you can, too.

Know Thy Customer

It's time to do a little prospecting. There are many companies out there that don't know exactly who their customers are, and when they have customers, they never look over purchasing data to see what type of customer is buying and what exactly they are buying. And that's a BIG problem, because if they really knew what customers are buying and what that specific customer demographic was buying it, they could put together programs and strategies to sell more of that item to their customers. They could sell variations of the items, or items that are up-sells that would complement the items the customers are currently buying. As you review your customer data on a daily, weekly, monthly, and quarterly basis you will see where most of your sales are coming from. Once you have this information you will know where to place your marketing efforts.

In addition to knowing what is being sold, you would collect the data in such a way that you would know who it's being sold to. Who it's being sold to is very important because then you can sell more to them as individuals. That means that if you know that Joe is buying a particular item from you but Joe doesn't know you sell another item that complements that purchase, then he should be made aware of the other item through marketing. But in addition to knowing the actual person's purchasing habits, you need to also decide what *types* of people are buying your products. In other words, are they dentists? Are they doctors? Are they blue collar?

Are they white collar? Do you know their income level? Is anything glaring at you from the data that you can exploit to help make more sales, to help your sales force with prospecting, so you know where to put your marketing?

Never assume that you know who the customer is. And never assume what the customer wants to buy. You need to have data to prove these things. No matter what the industry, no matter what you do—from office cleaning, to car repair, to hair salons, to restaurants—you need to know what's selling and who's buying it. And once you know that, you can make smart moves by selling more of it to the actual people, by type, who are buying it. This way you don't have to pull your hair out guessing. You have it in front of you. It's your company's actual sales data.

But many companies don't collect this type of data. They feel it's an intrusion on their customer; asking for zip codes and asking for e-mail addresses. But remember, when you collect the information, you do better than your competitors that don't. You also sell your goods and services to people who actually want it.

Now, keep in mind, too, that if you get only 5 to 10 percent of the people to give you the information that is good start. Ninety-five percent of them can say no for now. But it's your job to try to get at least 5 to 10 percent of customer data out of them. If they feel uncomfortable giving an e-mail address, maybe get a cell phone number. If they feel uncomfortable giving you their mailing address, get an e-mail. Get a regular phone number. Get their work address. Whatever. Get something. So get going, and get this important information from your customers so you can re-market to them and aquire more just like them.

Check If Your Marketing Is Working

So how do you figure out if your marketing is making a return on investment? Let's say you ran an ad in a newspaper, and the newspaper ad cost you $1,000. Let's say your average ticket (your average sale), is $20. How many clients or customers do you have to get from that ad to break even? You need to get fifty customers, right? In many cases that might be asking a lot for that one ad.

Always consider the lifetime value (LTV) of a customer. LTV is how long a customer will continue to buy from you. Here is a basic example. If you are a local carpet cleaner and you get a new customer, the chances they will return again are high. If you have data showing that an average first time customer spends $100 and usually repeat buys, averaging a customer spend of $1,000 in the course of his or her lifetime, if you acquire one customer you made your money back, in the long term, by getting just one customer from that ad. If you placed an ad that cost you $1,000 and that netted you only five customers at $100.00 each don't think it did not work. If they stay with you then you make $4,000 or more profit over their lifetimes. Because many business owners do not know the LTV of a customer, they will think that advertising does not work.

You need to decide if your advertising is working based on reality. You need to make sure that things are working, and that it's working based on the true numbers. Remember, if you don't have systems in place to keep enticing the customer to come back and purchase and become a loyal customer, then don't do any advertising. You're wasting your money.

If you have a sales force, you can calculate your return on investment by creating specials and offers that you track. When you create a special offer for your sales force, make sure you do not release that offer in any other media. It must only be offered by the salesperson. This way you can track the revenue from the offer.

Whatever the promotion or offer, you need to ensure you can track everything: promotion effectiveness, media placement, sales, and so forth. If you want to save money on advertising and marketing, it is very important to track where your sales are coming from.

What If People Are Calling But Do Not Become Customers?

If your marketing is informative and people call but do not buy, they have still been identified as people who are interested in your goods or services, and they are now considered hot leads. Do everything to get them into your marketing system, on your e-mail and direct mail list. You should follow up with them often. You should target them with phone calls from your sales force. And if it doesn't work out, you take them off your list, and then they go onto the cold prospect list. The cold prospect list is not aggressively marketed to, but you might send them an e-mail or letter from time to time. If you are finding that many people are calling but are not becoming customers, there is a problem with your advertisement or internal sales team that needs to be corrected immediately. You might also consider asking the people who call and do not buy why they decided to pass on your offer. This will extend the conversation and allow you to try to fix the problem in real time and maybe turn them into a customer.

Offers

In all your marketing, no matter what it is—ads, brochures, sell sheets, websites—whatever that first touch is, you should make your offer as fantastic as possible. You might need to put together an offer that will not make any money on the first sale. Offer things like a "100% Money Back, No Questions Asked" guarantee to take the risk out of doing business with you. This helps to gain the trust of the client, and it takes away all of the client's objections to doing business with you if he or she is on the fence. Very few people will actually take you up on the offer of the return or their money back.

Think about this logically for a second. I know offering

a 100% Money Back Guarantee is a big step for a lot of you reading this book. But if I purchased something from you and I was very unhappy with it and wanted to return it, would you give me my money back? For most of you, the answer would be absolutely yes. So then, why don't you just promote it? How often does it happen? If it happens a lot, you might want to reevaluate the situation and see if the services or products you're selling are up to par. But if currently people do not ask for a refund often, it'll probably happen just as infrequently if you make it public, and it will make a great risk-reversal offer. I believe there's only good that will come from it.

Your offer could also be a bundling of your products or services. It could also be a buy-one-get-one-free offer. Or buy one get the second half price. The offer must be something great to turn your prospects into customers. The purpose of the offer is to get new customers who can be marketed to over and over.

USP – Unique Selling Proposition

Before you engage in any marketing and advertising, it is of paramount importance to develop your Unique Selling Proposition (USP). A USP is probably the most important tactic of them all. It is what separates you from your competitors and helps customers with their decision to switch brands.

Perform a competitive analysis and then once you know what your competitors are doing answer this question from the point of view of your prospect. Why should I do business with you over all of my other choices?

To use an overused but strong example is Domino's Pizza: "You get fresh, hot pizza delivered to your door in 30 minutes or less—or it's free." They were the first to make such a claim and it is probably the reason they grew so fast.

Once you are clear that your USP is truly unique and of significant importance to your prospect, then and only then will you promote it.

To sign up for free marketing information, or to contact me, visit my website at www.thomasforgione.com

CHAPTER 5

The Difference Between Traditional And Digital Marketing

Once upon a time, there was a distinct difference between traditional and digital marketing and advertising, but now it's all under one umbrella of marketing. I'll still break down the old differences.

Traditional marketing would be direct mail; advertising in newspapers, magazines, and billboards; and advertising specialties that you give to your clients as gifts or ways for them to remember you. It could be a calculator with your name on it. It is also radio and television and any of the old media. There are also coupon magazines, trade show magazines, and related rags and flyers that are sent to you in the mail, or hung on a board in a supermarket, and so forth. Those are traditional means of advertising. The list really goes on and on.

Digital advertising is different. Digital advertising's job is to attract people in the digital world. These include websites, website banner advertising, pay per click, social media, e-mail blasts, Internet radio, podcasts, online videos, and so on, that are designed to get people to your website or other digital presence.

There are many differences between digital and traditional. Nothing in my experience would indicate that one is better than the other. It all boils down to, "Where are your customers? Who are your customers? What is the message you're going to produce and present to your customers? Will they respond?"

I like using a mix of terrestrial and digital marketing. There's no exact formula for what's going to work for you. You need to be sure that whatever type of marketing you decide to employ for your business, you must test. You must make sure that it's working before you spend more money on it. You must test, you must tweak, you must test, and then you must tweak again. You keep testing and tweaking until you run out of ways to make it better.

To sign up for free marketing information, or to contact me, visit my website at www.thomasforgione.com

CHAPTER 6

Website Design

A website must be an integral part of every business's marketing mix today. Not having a website is like not having a business card. You need to have a website in order to be successful and competitive in today's marketplace. There are many companies out there that still do not have a website. It's a shame because I'm sure their competitors are killing them because of this. What type of company will benefit from a website? Any company that wants to promote their services easily and affordably to their prospects. When the web first started, websites were defined as brochure and e-commerce. The brochure type of website just promotes who you are and what you do, like a printed brochure. Then there are e-commerce components that in addition to brochure-type features also give people the ability to download something or make a product purchase through a shopping cart or other means. But today it's all technically e-commerce.

A website is probably the least expensive

form of advertising there is. You can update it anytime you want. You can add specials to it. You could drive traffic to it through paid and free marketing. People can visit it twenty-four hours a day. It's like having a salesperson available all day, twenty-four hours a day, seven days a week to help promote and sell your products and services. You need to think of your website as a 24-hour salesperson with a cash register. You need to clearly identify what you want your website to do before you design it.

When considering the design of your website, keep in mind that people don't have time to wait around for slow loading, multimedia extravaganzas with a lot of flash, video and audio that loads immediately, people who walk out of the bottom of your website and start talking to you, or imagery that's nonsensical. You've all seen these types of websites. It's just nonsense. It's not what people are there for.

People are there to get information that will benefit them, so that's what you give them. Why would you ever want to go to a website and see a presentation with music and movement that is not important to the visitor? Get rid of that stuff. If you want to display video that demonstrates your products or shares testimonials, those are good uses. But nonsensical multimedia is just a waste of time, and all it does is show how great your web designer is. It doesn't help your customers, and your customers will disconnect from your message.

TACTIC #1

WEBSITE DESIGN

Know The Goal Of Your Website

Your website should be designed to encourage visitors to make a sale or take some other action you deem valuable. A goal could be to get customers on a website and have them fill out a contact form. If your goal is to get somebody to the website, get them to read some information, and from there to buy something and check out, that's another goal. You can set goals in your analytic program (a program designed to display the activity of your website; number of visitors, time on site, etcetera.), and it will show you how many goals you've achieved.

Your website theme should not be so over the top that when people go to your website they think, "Wow, what a beautiful website," or "This is a killer website." You blew it, because the reason they are there should be to buy something or get information, not to say how great your web person is. (Unless of course you are a website designer). Their eyes are off the prize. They're looking at the wrong thing. It would be nice to get the accolades such as, "Hey, I love your website," but you want them to buy something or contact you. Make sure your site is professional and fast loading, not over the top with too many bells and whistles.

If you have more than one item blinking on a page, you went too far. I've seen some websites where there are things blinking within the text. You keep trying to read the text and your eyes keep going to the stupid blinking thing, so you keep losing your place in the text. Try it. If it happens to you, it's happening to a lot of people. You have to be really careful of what little bells and whistles you put on a website. No music on load. That's a web annoyance. If they can't find that off button fast, they're going to back out of the website. Then you just lost a potential customer. Then you wonder why your cash register's not ringing.

TACTIC #2

WEBSITE DESIGN

Use Text Links Properly

You want visitors to know how to get around your website and get back to things so make sure you create easy to understand navigation and text links. When using text links make sure that when you code your text link color, the text link color is one color and the visited link color is a different color. The one thing you shouldn't do is make the text link color the same color as the text that's not linkable. Don't underline anything to emphasize it, because most people think that an underlined word is a link. Use underlines for real links so people can get to what they are looking for.

When a visitor hovers their cursor over a link, it should change color so they know it's a link. To spruce things up, you can design the site so that when people click the link, it changes color. Usually a hover will display the underline or not, but then when customer actually clicks on the word, it changes color. Keep your link color sequence the same on every page.

TACTIC #3

WEBSITE DESIGN

What Do You Want Visitors To Do On Your Website?

Do you want people to buy something? Do you want people to contact you? Do you want people to go into an automated sales funnel where an e-mail autoresponder will automatically follow up with prewritten sales information? Do you want them to sign up for your blog? What do you want to happen? What is the ultimate goal of the website?

Now most of you will say, "I want all that." Did you ever hear the saying, "You can do anything, but you can't do everything." You have to really focus on

NOTES

what is important to your visitor.

If you are redesigning an existing website, do not do anything until you review the analytics of your existing website. What is this site doing? Or what is it not doing that it should be doing? Are the goals being achieved? If you set up your goals properly analytics will tell you.

All pages of the website should clearly show who you are and where your website visitors are. A natural approach to this would be to make sure there's a logo on every page in the same spot. You don't want a website where one page looks one way and another page looks totally different.

People get confused very easily on websites; the more confusion, the more visitors will abandon shopping carts and click the back button to exit your site. They will just go away and might never return. You need to keep a consistent branded theme. Keep your logo on all pages in the same place as many people don't come into your website through the home page. They might come in through a search engine that only has your contact page or another internal page listed, and if the logo's not somewhere prominent, they're not going to know whose page they're on.

If your logo does not clearly identify what your company does then it's important to put a slogan or some sort of a tag line under the logo explaining your business. Don't do a double whammy and have a cryptic logo and a tag line that doesn't mean anything.

TACTIC #4

WEBSITE DESIGN

Choosing A Domain Name

Always try to get your company domain name, example, thomasforgione.com. If it is not available, there are many domain name extensions available as of this writing. Always try to secure a ".com" then go for the others. If the ".com" is not available make sure that when a person goes to the ".com" address registered it does not lead them to your competitor. If you can afford it then you should get as many domain name extensions with your company name as possible.

You could get a keyword domain name, for example, www.productname.com. You should try to keep it short, understandable, and easy to spell.

You can also register many different domain names to use in your marketing. You could send them to the same website or a special landing page, but make sure you tell the search engines you only want one website to be listed. You do this through the use of redirects.

Don't forget if your company serves a language other than English you can secure that domain name in that language as well.

TACTIC #5

WEBSITE DESIGN

Copywriting

The text that visitors read is called copy. It's best to have it written by a professional copywriter. But no matter who does it, make sure you spell-check, grammar check, and fact-check.

Don't be afraid to include a lot of copy about products or services because the more information you provide the better. Since your website is an online salesperson, it needs to answer the questions visitors would have if they were speaking to a salesperson. This will help them make a decision to buy from you. I'm not saying that you should have twenty pages of copy, but don't be afraid to go long, within reason. It should be easy to understand.

You shouldn't use dry, academic speech in your copy. It should be so easy to read that a fifth grader could do it. It should be intriguing. It should give people what they're there for; that is, it should engage them. It should explain in detail how they'll benefit from doing business with you.

What's your unique selling proposition? Ask this question of yourself. Why would I do business with you over all my other choices? That has to be explained in your text, imagery, videos, and so forth. You've got to be better than the competition, or else. You don't want to be close to the competition. You want to be better.

NOTES

Most websites fail at this. What they do is promote how great the company is, how great the owner is, and that's bad. Tell them how you and your products and services will serve them. When you're writing copy for your website, make sure it's customer centric, not company centric. Your company-centric copy can go on the About Us page. Don't worry; you'll have a chance to brag, but it should be on the About Us page only. An example of company ego is where a website trumpets, "We're great! We've been in business a long time! We love ourselves! We have a big staff. We have the best solutions. All of our customers are very happy. We provide prompt attention to all our customers." Yadda, yadda, yadda. Big deal.

Stay away from sarcasm. Usually people know you're being sarcastic by your tone when you actually say something. But in copy it's hard to do that, and if they can't tell you're joking, then you're not joking. Be careful.

If you have a lot of copy, use visual elements that will help the eye move down the page; use images that are related to the content, subheads, bullets, tables, and so forth.

When using headlines, make sure you get the entire point across in the headline. Many people will only read a headline, and if it does not grab them they will move on.

When possible, use captions under your images because they are also valuable when people skim read. Also, if you need to make an announcement or have something very important to say always do it under an image. Some people will read the headline, look at the image, and read the caption, and that's all they'll do.

Use sans serif fonts like Arial for body text. Stay away from serif fonts. Avoid backgrounds that don't have a high contrast to the text. Even though black and yellow are high contrast, don't use them. That combination of text and background is hard on the eyes. Try to use white or light backgrounds with black or very dark color text.

TACTIC #6

WEBSITE DESIGN

If Visitors Don't Speak Your Language

Let's say you need to have foreign languages on your website. What do you do? You could use Google Translate. If you have WordPress, you can get the Google Translate plug-in where visitors can select their language.

If you're not using a CMS (content management system) that will allow the use of translation software and are just trying to give the customer the gist of what you sell, then there's an easy solution. (Always have someone who speaks the non-dialect version of the language.) Create two or three paragraphs of what your company is about and place the pages on your website in those languages. Make sure in the copy that you let visitors know when the person who speaks that language is going to be at your store or office. Use the language for the links as well. For example don't use the words "We speak Spanish". Use the words hablamos español.

We did that for a company years ago. They had Italian, Hebrew, French, Spanish, and German versions of a little paragraph about what they did, and the site noted when the people who could understand those languages would be there. Most of the people who called loved it even though they knew some English. They liked being accommodated. That's an easy way to do it, instead of getting a whole website translated.

TACTIC #7

WEBSITE DESIGN

Call-To-Action Images

Your website should also have tactical ways to grab people's attention in addition to great copywriting. You should have images that sole purpose is to promote a call to action (CTA). These are images dispersed throughout the website that instructs visitors on what to do. "Click here to download this report." "Click here to contact us." "Click here to chat with a sales representative." "Click here to read our testimonials." Don't be afraid to use the words "click here."

People need to be guided. They need to know what to do. When you make the assumption that people understand what to do on your website, you're blowing it. Most people don't know what to do, especially on a website they've never been to before. Give them guidance by using calls to action. Incorporate whatever you think will help get people to the important content of the website, the content you need them to read or watch, so they can make a decision to do business with your company. DON'T EXPECT VISITORS WILL KNOW WHAT TO DO. MOST WILL NOT.

TACTIC #8

WEBSITE DESIGN

Make It Easy To Contact You

You need contact forms and phone numbers all over your website. I believe that a contact form or quick contact should be on every page of your website. No matter where they are, no matter what they're reading, if they have the inkling to contact you, they could put it right into a contact form and you'll get it via e-mail. Or you could set it up to be texted to you, or they can click on your phone number and either dial it if they're looking at it with their cell phone, or they can make a phone call right away. Don't make them hunt for the contact information. You want them to get to it fast.

TACTIC #9

WEBSITE DESIGN

Your Website Must Load Fast

Too many images and multimedia will make your website load slowly. You want a website to load within four seconds, or else visitors will leave. It's so easy to hit the back button and go to your competition, so you want your web pages to load as quickly as possible. If you don't think four seconds is a long time, get your watch out and time four seconds. Sing the classic "Happy Birthday" song. That's about ten seconds.

TACTIC #10

WEBSITE DESIGN

Your Images Must Be Relatable To The Demographic You Serve

The images that you use on your website need to be consumer-related or company related. For example, let's say you have a company that sells landscaping. You wouldn't want to use images of your trucks on that site. You will use images of your typical consumers, smiling next to their beautiful lawn. If they're thirty-five to sixty years old, married with children, with a regular ranch-style house with a decent lawn, that's the picture you put on your website. Don't put a mansion on your website with people dripping with jewelry, and don't use weird imagery on your site. Try to mirror your actual customer on your website. You'll do that in all other places you advertise in as well.

TACTIC #11

WEBSITE DESIGN

Let Your Customers Brag About You

Get customer testimonials and put them on your website. You should have written and video testimonials. Video testimonials are fantastic; just make sure they don't look overproduced. Grab a smartphone camera and take some pictures and videos of your clients telling everybody how great you are.

I had a person call me about three or four days before one of my speaking engagements. She wasn't a client yet. She said, "I saw your name on a flyer for the seminar, and I went to your website and I saw so many testimonials, I had to call you. I knew you were the one." OK. I said, "Well, didn't you look at my work, too?" She said, "Yeah, I looked at your beautiful work, but then when I saw those testimonials, that sold me on you." Get as many testimonials as you can.

Some people are fearful and don't want to ask their customers to do a video or a written testimonial. They feel like they're imposing, which is ridiculous because if you gave your customer good service, they'll be happy to give you a testimonial. In fact, when I e-mail people back after they ask me something, they say, "Thank you." I say, "You're welcome. Your testimonials are always welcome." You need to do this. Testimonials help prospects turn into customers as they provide "social proof" and do some of the selling for you.

TACTIC #12

WEBSITE DESIGN

Give Them Something Of Value For Free

If possible, you should also have downloadable reports or special offers on your website whereby you capture potential customers' information in exchange for the report or offer. You should create downloadable information that is valuable to your prospect. It could be about your industry or your products or just a great offer or coupon. Depending on your industry you could have "how to" areas of your website. People like to share videos with their friends, when they do your marketing goes a lot further. Especially when they share it on social media.

TACTIC #13

WEBSITE DESIGN

Navigation

Your website must have logical navigation in the same spot on every page. Navigation is a button or text links for Products, Services, Contact Us, About Us, FAQs, Testimonials, and so forth.

Your navigation scheme—the way it is laid out—should be logical. The first button should always be the goal. In other words, if I get someone to my website and I want them to learn about what I sell, I'm not going to put "About the company" first. I'm going to put what I want them to buy as the first item. Make it easy.

Don't put the "About the Company" first. Nobody cares about who you are. They only care about what's in it for them. If they are first time visitors they

NOTES

are rarely there for an education about your company. "About the company" needs to be there because once I like your product or service offering, I'm going to check you out. The site should always be set up to be customer centric. Even in the navigation: customer centric, not company centric—no company ego.

Visitors might want to learn about your company. Some care about that, BUT it should only be there after they decide you can give them what they want. Most visitors only want to know if you have the product or service they need. Do you have the trip I need to book? The cruise I need to go on? The computer I need to buy? That's what most visitors care about.

TACTIC #14

WEBSITE DESIGN

Keep It Simple And Easy To Read

When you are creating your navigation, don't be cryptic. If you have products, don't say "offerings." When you have services, don't say "ways we can help." Don't confuse people. Get them right there. Say "our products" and "our services." Don't make visitors guess, because when they keep guessing and getting it wrong they give up and leave your website.

You don't want to spend money on marketing to get people to the website and then make them confused or angry because they can't find what they are looking for. Keep it simple. Make the navigation font size large; try for a fourteen, fifteen, or sixteen-point font. Don't go with Arial ten. Those days are long gone. Make it large and easy to read. Try to keep navigation down to seven or eight main areas. Anything more and visitors might get confused.

TACTIC #15

WEBSITE DESIGN

Only Publish Pages With Content

No website page should ever be "under construction". It is not good for your search engine listings and it doesn't serve the visitor. Don't publish a page with the guy with a jackhammer or little dog with the helmet running by, dragging the "Under Construction" sign. No one cares what you plan to do in the future. Leave the page off the website if it is not ready for publishing.

TACTIC #16

WEBSITE DESIGN

Search Box

You should always consider the addition of a search box. Most content management programs have built-in search engines, so there's no reason not to have it. Most shopping carts out of the box have some sort of search feature. That's the first thing many visitors look for.

If you have a large site, you should have an advanced search feature because some search functions are too broad and result in a large amount of results; an advanced search will help them narrow them down. If you have a shopping cart, people might enjoy searching by price or reviews.

TACTIC #17

WEBSITE DESIGN

Mobile Websites

Your website must be viewable on mobile devices, including tablets and whatever new type of viewing device comes out. For quite some time now, tablets have outsold PCs in the United States because they are a very convenient way to surf the web, getting information without having to boot up a computer.

If your website can't be seen clearly on a smartphone, you wasted some of your advertising money because many will view your website on a smartphone or other mobile device.

Many companies are using QR (quick response) codes for people to scan and to get more information about their company. They use a QR code scanner and guess what? It's done on a cell phone. You don't want to promote that you have a QR code or are using QR codes and then have a website that's only designed for a computer screen and not a cell phone. You just wasted your time. You wasted your money. And what did you do? You made the customer experience go into the trash. It was a bad experience.

Customers might think, "Well, if they don't even care enough about us to make a mobile site so we can get access to the product, how are they going to treat us as a customer?" If you think that people don't think those kinds of things, then maybe you shouldn't be in business. Those things are important, and they need to be addressed immediately. Imagine that your customer is on the road and trying to access directions to your restaurant only to find that she can't get to your site's contact, location, or directions page because it's not mobile friendly. It happens all the time and you've lost customers. If you've surfed the web on a smartphone, it's happened to you. If it happens to you, it's going to happen to many other people.

You should never create a website, mobile or not, thinking that everyone has the best, fastest modem and the quickest computer; you're going to hurt yourself. Always plan on a slow computer and mobile device; test your site on those devices and make sure that it can be seen within one or two seconds. It's very easy to do. There are mobile page-loading simulators on the web.

TACTIC #18

WEBSITE DESIGN
A/B Split Testing

A/B split testing is when you create two separate pages. (You can perform A/B testing for free with Google Experiments.) You put code in both versions of your web pages, and it will serve different pages to visitors. Then you'll be able to track which page was more effective in getting people to where you want them to go. This way you can determine which page layout works best to convert visitors into customers.

TACTIC #19

WEBSITE DESIGN

Search Engine Optimization

Search engine optimization (SEO) is very important, BUT it should be thought out before hiring a website designer or copywriter. You need a strong idea as to who your website will be for, before creating it. The copy will use industry keywords and phrases actual visitors will be using when searching for a product or service that a company like yours provides. Be careful not to stuff keywords into existing website copy to increase your SEO as it usually makes the text read poorly.

Since SEO techniques change frequently, here are some guidelines that work for me:

1) Always use keywords and phrases that you are sure your visitors are searching for. But don't over use them. Write for your visitors not for the search engines. You can check this by using Google and other keyword tools.

2) Every page will have specific keywords and phrases related to the content on the page. This is also true for the image tags. If I'm on your chocolate chip cookie page, you should not waste space in your tags with keywords that relate to ice cream. Keep all unrelated phrases to a minimum in the actual text as well.

3) Every page will have a unique description tag related to the content of the page.

4) Include your main keyword (a keyword specific to the exact content of the page it's on) or phrase in the title tag and the description of your page.

5) Include the same main keyword or phrase within the first heading <h1> tag on your page.

6) Include the same main keyword or phrase within the first sentence of the first paragraph of the page.

7) All graphics ALT tags, titles, and captions will have the main keyword within them. They will also describe the image.

NOTES

8) All pages should have a minimum of three hundred words.

9) Use ethical link building. If you are a member of a trade organization, make sure their website has your website address on it. Any related websites should also have your link on them. Don't ask websites that are high trafficked and that you have nothing to do with to add your link. Your back links should come from sites that are related to your content.

10) Ensure your website has a lot of high quality, industry specific content.

11) Don't use techniques that will get you banned from the search engines. Just search for banned SEO techniques and you will find many that you should stay away from.

TACTIC #20

WEBSITE DESIGN

Getting Fast, Qualified Traffic To Your Website

Do not wait for the search engines to bring you quality visitors. Many companies put their website online and expect search engine miracles to happen. They expect the search engines to find you in a few days and then be in a great first page position in the organic search engine results with the hopes of it bringing them enough traffic to make a significant amount of sales. This does not happen. In addition to search engines you should surf the web and find quality places to advertise. Keep in mind that this is not a quick fix and that it takes a strong effort to make sure your website is placed in the correct places. If not, the traffic you receive will be unqualified. It's like advertising your hair salon in an auto shopping guide. It might get some traffic but the demographic you're looking for might not be reading this website.

You can also contribute to blogs and online forums where your customer types (demographics) are served. You can reply to popular blog posts with great information. People who read it will look at your profile and will check you out. Make sure your profile is 100 percent complete and includes your website address BEFORE you start responding.

TACTIC #21

WEBSITE DESIGN

Include Your Website Address On All Advertisements And Materials

Place your website address in every piece of advertising and marketing you do. This point is overlooked by many companies. They either don't put the site in their advertising or they make it so small that it is almost impossible to read. Your company website is the least expensive form of advertising. You should be telling everyone about it every day. Don't end a conversation without letting people know about it.

Don't forget to place you website

address on your letterhead, business cards, envelopes, invoices, advertising specialties, T-shirts, baseball caps, pens, business checks, and so forth.

To sign up for free marketing information, or to contact me, visit my website at www.thomasforgione.com

CHAPTER 7

Content Marketing

Content marketing is when you create information that is consumed by prospects to help them make a decision to become your customer. Give them a great education with the information, so great they could take it and go anywhere else, maybe even do it themselves. The more content you give them, the better position you will be in. You will become more of an expert in their eyes.

TACTIC #22

CONTENT MARKETING

Great Content Turns Suspects Into Informed Prospects

A great technique for websites, if you're trying to capture customers' attention, is to give them as much free stuff as possible. Let them keep consuming your free stuff, because while they're reading it, where are they? On your website.

Personally, I give marketing articles and marketing techniques on my website. I try to give as much as I can, and they can take my information and go somewhere else, but they usually call me.

To give you an idea, I tweet marketing techniques. I post marketing techniques on Facebook, LinkedIn, and blogs, and I speak at seminars where I give marketing techniques and strategies. Some of which I have video recorded so I can post the video. I'm constantly giving content, and so should you. Let's say you're a bartending school and you're trying to get people to attend your bartending school. What do you do? Don't just say, "Hey, we're the best bartending school in town. We'll make sure you'll get those drinks perfect every time." No, you should give them some recipes. Give them some video instruction. Give them some free stuff so they may say, "Wow, these guys must be good. They're giving it away. I have to call them and see what I'm not getting." Make sure you tell your visitors, "This content is free. By the way, if you would like to learn additional stuff then enroll, or if you'd like to join our membership site where you get more

NOTES

NOTES

information, then join, or if you'd like to get updated information periodically to your e-mail box, sign up for our e-mail list."

TACTIC #23

CONTENT MARKETING

Here Is An Option If You Don't Like Writing

There are professionals ghost writers who will write the content for you. Everything from simple blog articles to long reports and books. They could be expensive, but remember that you get what you pay for. You have to make sure that it wasn't something that they wrote for someone else and are now reselling it to you. You don't want that, so you have to have them sign a document that says, "If we find that you've done this for someone else, we're not only going to want our money back, but we're going to sue you for this amount of money." (Check with your Lawyer about this first.) Have a really strong contract.

It would be best if you or a staff member

could write the information yourself. It doesn't have to be five-hundred-word articles. You should have some longer information, but most of them should be two or three paragraph blog articles. Articles need to be related to the overall content; if you own a bartending school write about bartending.

To sign up for free marketing information, or to contact me, visit my website at www.thomasforgione.com

NOTES

CHAPTER 8

Creating A Lead-Generation Campaign

You need to do everything possible to collect leads. A lead is a visitor that has raised their hand and said I am interested in what you are selling. It is always best to market to people who have a strong interest in your company and its products and services.

TACTIC #24

CREATING A LEAD-GENERATION CAMPAIGN

Give Your Visitors An Offer They Can't Refuse

Create a report or downloadable PDF; it can be a white paper, or it can be information related to your industry, for example, "Seven tips to choosing the right mattress" or "The seven ways to make sure you choose the right lawyer." It could be anything, but it has to be of high value. It has to be something that people want to actually read, watch, or listen to. That's the most important first step. You can research your topics on the web. You could also visit online book stores to see the most popular bestselling book topics to gather ideas.

It doesn't have to be *War and Peace*, but it should be long enough that they get good information, and make sure you're giving them something they could use whether they do business with you or not. Also make it shareable, so they will share it with others thus expanding your marketing reach. If you are creating a booklet that is available for download, you want to make sure that it has your branding all over it and the content shows your expertise. You want to make sure that you are presented as an expert in your field.

NOTES

65

TACTIC #25

CREATING A LEAD-GENERATION CAMPAIGN

Direct Visitors To A Squeeze Page

Once you create your content or offer, you would then create a squeeze page or sign-up page. The best thing to do is to create a squeeze page; you've seen them. At the top of the page it has either imagery or a video explaining why they should download the PDF or whatever they're getting. Then on the right side there's a sign-up form for their name and e-mail.

I've seen sign-up forms that have name, address, city, state, zip, e-mail, phone, blood type—it's crazy. The more fields you put on there, the fewer people will fill them out. It would be nice to get all that information about them, but this isn't the place to do it. This is just to get their e-mail address and their name. Once you do that, you have a qualified prospect. Sometimes it's best to not allow an immediate download. Have it available after they opt into your e-mail list. It will be on the "thank you

for opting in" page or sent to them via
email after confirmation. This way you
know you have a valid e-mail address on
your list. Most of the e-mail deployment
companies can do this.

Remember that when you're using an
e-mail service, you set it up so people
who go for this download or product
are put into a special list. That list has
been configured by you to send out
autoresponder e-mails on a daily,
one-week, or two-week schedule, so you
add ten or fifteen autoresponder e-mails
into the system. Then when the visitors
signs up and is placed on the list, it
triggers the autoresponder sequence.

There are a few different ways to get people to your offer or information.

One way is to create a separate website
that's not on your main domain. You
could place ads on Facebook, Google,
Yahoo, Bing, or other sites to promote
your offer. Always explain why they
should download your information or
offer, etcetera. Once they do that starts
the process.

You could advertise in TV commercials, on the radio, and in print. You can do an e-mail blast to your existing customers, or you can do promoted posts and advertising on social media. There are many places to advertise your offer, but the point is you need to get qualified traffic to it. You can also create a blog article to generate traffic. You can also promote it through other blogs and bloggers and forums. There are plenty of ways to get traffic, but you need to get qualified traffic.

Once they acquire your information they are qualifying themselves. If the ad warns people to read your information before hiring an attorney, a person is not going to click on that looking for chocolate chip cookie recipes. You qualify them solely by the ad content. They click on the ad and go to your website where you've already set up your autoresponders and your e-mail service so when they sign up they are now in your marketing system.

In addition to autoresponders, you can incorporate a direct mail campaign. But you need the prospects postal address to do it. You create letters (four, five, or six) that would go out to the same group of prospects as a drip campaign using traditional snail mail. Depending on your industry and to save some money, you could use postcards. Letters sometimes outperform postcards depending on the industry, so do your research.

To sign up for free marketing information, or to contact me, visit my website at www.thomasforgione.com

CHAPTER 9

Squeeze Page

A squeeze page is a one-page website designed to allow your visitors to enter their email and name in exchange for something they deem valuable such as an offer, report or other content.

TACTIC #26

SQUEEZE PAGE

Keep Your Squeeze Page Simple

They go to this page, read your information, sign up with their name and e-mail, and then they get the offer. By entering their contact information and clicking the button, they're taken to a page that explains what to do next, which should tell them they will receive a confirmation e-mail to confirm. After confirmation they will be directed to, or emailed the offer. This two-step authentication process is used so you know it's a valid e-mail address.

Most people who are reasonable will understand that the trade-off is to give their email and name for the offer, and they will subscribe if they're interested. The great thing is if they're not interested and they don't, that's great, because you don't want to market to people who don't want to listen anyway.

Why Should You Create A Squeeze Page?

Many visitors to a website do not make a purchase or inquiry on their first visit. There could be many reasons: they are researching before buying; they stumbled upon your website from a link on another website and are not in the research stage; they landed on your site via a friend's urging; they might be on your website by accident. But if they are ready to buy and are not buying from you, it could be because they simply don't know your company well enough to trust you.

Getting people to download your report or offer gives the visitor information about your products or services and allows you to market to them frequently. By signing up for your free information, you're developing a hot lead list.

To sign up for free marketing information,
or to contact me, visit my website at
www.thomasforgione.com

CHAPTER 10

Landing Pages

Landing pages are the big brother of squeeze ages. They are designed to give specific content to potential customers. The landing page doesn't give them the whole website; it gives them just a very specific look at the product or service that they're researching or intending to buy. The reason you do this is quite simply, "to only give them what they are currently interested in."

TACTIC #27

LANDING PAGES

Keep The Message Hyper-Focused

Let's say you're a landscaper. You want to promote your grass-cutting services. You don't put information on your landing page related to anything else because you're trying to get grass cutting customers, maybe as a foot-in-the-door or "loss leader"; eventually you could sell them more stuff, but right now you just

73

want to get people who are interested in getting their grass cut. Why take them to a page that confuses them and explains all the other things that you do. It's a very fast-food society that we live in today, and we don't want to promote everything to everyone especially if we're driving traffic to the website through search engine results or some banner ad that's specific to the content of a website landing page.

Keep it simple, keep it focused, and make sure that a landing page has the following components. The first thing is professionally written, benefit-based, hyper-focused sales copy whose sole purpose is to get people from the beginning to the end with calls to action in between. It should be customer-centric copy that talks about the benefits of doing business with you, buying your services or products, and so forth. Don't use the less-is-more scenario. If your customers want more, you want them to be able to read more. The more they read and the more information they see, the better the prospect they will be. You also want to include testimonials for your company, product, or service. As you already learned, you want to make sure that your copy is not dry and academic, but is easy to understand. It should be broken up with visual elements; you can use some imagery, tables, and color to make it more appealing and easy to read. You want to give users a quick but thorough education about your product or service so they take an action, contact you via a web form, or call you.

You should have multiple ways for them to contact you all over your landing pages. There should be either sign-up forms or download-free reports, quick contact forms, and buy-now buttons. It should be all over that site. A landing page doesn't have to be one page. It could be a few pages but it still has to be hyper-focused on the subject matter. Try not to have more than three pages, unless absolutely necessary.

Landing pages should be tracked with analytics (visitor tracking). Every single thing that can be tracked on the landing page should be tracked. If you're going to put money into advertising and driving traffic to it through pay per click or banner ads, you want to make sure that you have a very good analytic program. Google Analytics is free. It will give you

NOTES

more than enough data to see if your landing page is working or not.

As with anything you produce online landing pages should also be A/B split tested. You create two versions of your landing page then you track and see which one converts visitors. The one that converts the best is the one that you're going to ultimately use. There are some schools of thought that the second landing page should be completely different, and some say, you should change just the headline and a few elements so you know what worked. That's totally up to you because you don't have to test just once. Google has free tools with which you can do A/B split testing. Landing pages should be created based on the type (demographic) of customer you're looking for.

To sign up for free marketing information, or to contact me, visit my website at www.thomasforgione.com

CHAPTER 11

Marketing Automation

Marketing automation has been around for quite a while, and there are different types. With marketing automation, you create a system of actions. For example, a visitor comes to the website, clicks a link, goes to a contact form or free report sign-up, and enters data into the form. Now we have their contact information, and based on their actions we have a system that performs automated marketing tasks.

TACTIC #28

MARKETING AUTOMATION

Create An Automatic Follow Up System

The prospect could be followed up with a telephone call or an e-mail that are part of your sequence of marketing steps. They might be put into a drip campaign, which sends them a sequence of e-mails they would get over the course of two or three days, weeks, or months via a triggered or scheduled autoresponder.

An easy way to figure out what to put into your autoresponder message is if you currently have a sales process, talk to your top salespeople about the steps that clients normally go through before they make a purchase. See if you could automate the marketing to duplicate those steps or move those steps along faster to help you sell faster. You don't have to use autoresponders; you can also do it with letters and postcards. They can go into a system of automation. You just have to make sure that the system makes sense for your company.

TACTIC #29

MARKETING AUTOMATION

Make It Personal

Personalization is a great tactic. Instead of saying, "Dear whoever," or "Dear friend," you say "Dear Joe," "Dear Mary," "Dear Peter"; use their name in the personalization. You can use personalization in many places on an e-mail. You place their name throughout the e-mail where it's grammatically correct.

There are many software programs out there that will help you. If you have a sales force, try to get software that is also a Customer Relationship Manager (CRM) as it forces salespeople to take the next step; follow up, make notes, and so forth. You want to have some marketing automation in place from the first touch of a potential customer all the way to the end.

As you are closing sales, they should be taken off the presales campaign and onto a different marketing automation sequence to create upsells and referrals. It seems like a lot of work, but once it's in place, it's automatic marketing. No matter what size company you are, you could do some form of marketing automation.

To sign up for free marketing information, or to contact me, visit my website at www.thomasforgione.com

NOTES

CHAPTER 12

Remarketing

There are many ways to define remarketing. Basically it is a way to bring your visitors back to your website by the use of ads or email.

TACTIC #30

REMARKETING

Guide Visitors Back To Your Website

These visitors may or may not have completed a specific goal you have defined. For example a visitor might place items in a shopping cart but did not check out. Then they visit another website and they see an ad promoting some or all of the items they have placed in their abandoned shopping cart or have viewed on your website.

It does not have to be just for shopping cart abandonment. It can be to promote your website if the visitor did not sign up for a webinar or report, etcetera. It can

NOTES

also just be used to remind them about your company when they are surfing other websites on the web. Did you ever visit a website and then see a promotion for that exact website on Facebook or another site? That is usually remarketing in action. Without getting too technical when a visitor goes to your website a tracking cookie is placed on their computer. This cookie is what is tracked and tells the website they are currently on what ad to display. Usually displaying branded static banners or videos.

To sign up for free marketing information, or to contact me, visit my website at www.thomasforgione.com

CHAPTER 13

E-Mail List Building

You want to collect as many e-mails as possible from your clients, your prospects, your suspects—whoever. You want to get as many people as you can onto an e-mail list who are interested in what you have to say or sell.

TACTIC #31

E-MAIL LIST BUILDING

Give Value To The "Right" Customers

Give people a strong reason to give their e-mail to you. Make sure you collect it from people who fall within your customer demographic and psychographic profile. When you're looking for suspects, you need them to fit within the profile you've determined is your best customer. You only want to go after your best customer and their e-mail addresses. You MUST incentivize them to give it to you. This actually happened to me. I went to a card store. I was at the checkout, and they said, "Do you have an e-mail?" I said, "Yes." That was the end of the conversation. It would have been better if she would have said, "Would you like to get specials or updates or information on how you can get this item on special sale?" If she had given me a little bit of why I should give the store my e-mail, she probably would have gotten it.

Even if you get ten out of a hundred to say yes, that's 10 percent. That's a great start but make your offer as strong as possible to ensure you get a higher percentage. Make sure that you send them the information as promised. In addition, let them know about other things that might interest them. You could also send them to your blog, as long as it's informative for the consumer. Let's say you have a list of ten thousand people on your e-mail list. You know that they're into horseback riding, and you happen to own a horseback-riding training company. You could say, "Hey, sign up here for this special, customer-only, online video training." You could

NOTES

charge them for access and then you will hear your cash register ringing…cha-ching!

You could buy an e-mail list, but it's not the greatest way to get a list. But if you must buy it, have the e-mail list company deploy and e-mail the list with a message from you. You could say, "Hey! This is who I am. This is what I write about and how it will benefit you. Just click here to sign up for my blog updates and specials." That link goes to your website sign-up page. This way you get followers, legitimately, people who really want to listen to you.

TACTIC #32

E-MAIL LIST BUILDING

Get Your Existing Customers Emails Without Asking

Now, let's take a company that has had paper receipts for years where they have the name, address, city, state, and zip of all their customers, but they never ask for their e-mail. You can call every one of

NOTES

them up and ask for their e-mail which is
time consuming. But I suggest you hire
a stenographer to come to your location
and type all the addresses into Excel, then
you can give your list to a list broker and
they will append e-mails to the addresses
they have in their universe and sell them
back to you. It's usually about a 10 to 15
percent of the total complete records.
So if you have a list of ten thousand
customers, you're going to get at least one
thousand e-mails out of that. How cool
is that?

**To sign up for free marketing
information, or to contact me,
visit my website at
www.thomasforgione.com**

CHAPTER 14

Social Media

Facebook, Twitter, Instagram, Pinterest, LinkedIn. Which one do you use? The answer is simple. Where are your customers and prospects? You should NOT assume that all of your customers are active on Facebook. Notice I said active? That is the secret. When you ask your customers what their favorite social media site is, you ask them how active they are. You might be surprised. Then, and only then, you start your plan of attack. You might think that using a company to manage your social media is a good idea. Personally, I think you or an in-house employee should perform the social media tasks.

TACTIC #33

SOCIAL MEDIA

Keep Your Social Media Activity Professional

Here are some basic rules to get you started (not in any particular order):

1) Consider social media as marketing. It should bring you an ROE (Return On Engagement).

2) Do everything ethically possible to build your following.

3) Do not BUY followers.

4) Never start posting on a social media sites until you look around and see what others are doing.

5) Do not pay to become a member unless you have researched and made sure it will bring you an ROE.

6) Your business presence should always be professional. Do not speak of your personal life unless this is in your overall plan.

7) Never include photos that would put you, your business, or your customers in a bad light.

8) Stay far away from any posts that contain political, sexual, racial, or religious content.

9) All of your posts and imagery should be created with sharing in mind.

10) Post often, more than once per day.

11) Do not sell, sell, sell. Instead educate, educate, educate, and then soft sell. Otherwise, people will become blind to your posts.

12) Use social media to build yourself as an expert.

13) Use professionally created images for your branding headers and logo.

14) Fill out all profiles to 100 percent.

15) Use logos for business pages and head shots for your personal page. However, if it is for a sales professional, physician, attorney, or something similar, I would use a professional head shot (not the one where you cut your ex out of the

picture).

16) Try the advertising programs offered and see if it generates sales.

17) Tie in blog articles, YouTube videos, and posts, but don't make them the main source of your posts.

18) If someone responds to a post, respond back within twenty-four hours. There is nothing worse than a one-sided conversation.

19) Only "like" things you truly like. Don't like just to be liked.

20) Don't violate the terms and conditions of the site.

21) Don't follow people just to get them to follow you back. Quality of followers is more important than quantity.

22) Don't invite followers to play games.

To sign up for free marketing information, or to contact me, visit my website at www.thomasforgione.com

CHAPTER 15

Pay Per Click Or Per Impression

Pay per click (PPC) is a great way for companies to get to the top of search engines fast. I will not go over all the details in this book simply because technology changes so quickly and the techniques might be outdated as soon as this book is printed.

TACTIC #34

PAY PER CLICK OR PER IMPRESSION

Pay Per Click And Pay Per Impression Is Fast And More Controlled

Companies that are serious about online marketing should strongly consider a PPC campaign and hire a professional or educate themselves before starting it. PPC is great because you have control over the qualified traffic that visits your website. You can set and bid for keyword phrases that people would search for, and your ad will only appear if those phrases are searched. Many factors determine the actual position of your ad within the results, so check each search engine carefully. For example, if you are an Italian restaurant, you would use the keyword phrase, "Italian restaurant." People search for that phrase, and your ad appears. They click the ad and go to your website, and then you are charged for the click. Prices for clicks vary, so be sure you stay within your budget.

There are other PPC opportunities besides search engines. There are social media sites, blogs, pre and post roll video (ads that appear before or after an on-line video), and other popular websites. Do not contract for any PPC unless you are absolutely sure your customer demographic is served and you have checked the references of others buying the exact same advertising.

Pay Per Impression is similar to PPC, but in this case you do not pay per click; you pay per one thousand impressions (the amount of times your banner ad is displayed). You have to determine if your CPM (cost per thousand) versus the conversion rate is worth the money.

To sign up for free marketing information,
or to contact me, visit my website at
www.thomasforgione.com

CHAPTER 16

Blogs And Blogging

A blog could be a daily account of things that are going on in a company. It could be things that you are doing personally; then it's a personal blog and might not be great for your business. It could be anything that you want to tell the public. It could be press releases. It could be new product launches, new company hires. Or it could be a support blog where you talk about products and services and how to fix them. It's really just content on the website that helps educate people to make an informed decision to do business with you. Blogging also helps you show your expertise.

TACTIC #35

BLOGS AND BLOGGING

Create Interesting Content For Your Visitors

A few of my rules about blogging come from my father, who owned a liquor store and bar for many years, always said there are a few things you don't talk about in a bar: anything related to sex, politics, race, religion, or personal attacks. I agree. You should stay away from those topics on your company blog as well. We don't want to know your beliefs or what you ate for dinner. We don't want to know when you went to the theater. We only want to know those things if you can relate it to me. We want to know, "What's in it for me?"

You want to have articles that are important to your customers and will explain to them what your products are all about, how they can use your products, how they will benefit our lives, what cool things they can do, how they'll make us thinner, happier, and healthier. Your blog should have articles and videos. It should have imagery to make it interesting. Put a video within the text with a product demonstration. It all helps.

You can have separate segments of your blog for company information such as movers and shakers, public relations, and press releases. That's fine, but make sure you categorize so I don't have to waste time figuring it out. Content should be in categories so I decide if I want to read about that subject if I choose to, but your main website blog should be about your products, your company, and your services and how they relate to me and how they will benefit me.

A blog should also be very fast loading, just like the rest of your website. It should allow the printing of your articles. It should allow people to share your articles on social media. Blogging software like WordPress has many free plug-ins that allow you to incorporate social sharing buttons on your website and blog. Make sure that you use them; sharing is very important.

NOTES

TACTIC #36

BLOGS AND BLOGGING

Allow Commenting

If you can monitor it, your blog should have commenting turned on. You want people to respond to some articles or blog posts you write, as long as you have the administrative control over the blog and can allow only comments that you've approved. The more people who are speaking on behalf of the article, the more hyper-focused content your blog is producing. You want to generate as much content as possible for your blog, and comments are great way to do it. You should encourage comments most of the time.

TACTIC #37

BLOGS AND BLOGGING

Use More Than Just Text

You should also include audio podcasts on your blog. People still download podcasts. They listen to them on their phone or iPod, but they also still burn them to CDs. Some listen to them while commuting to work. They listen to it on the train, on the plane, and on the boat, but a website should have the option if possible.

You should create your content as many ways as possible because you never know how someone would like to consume it. Lots of people will look at a video, but then there are other people who will want to read and not watch a video. Then there are people who want to listen and not watch a video or read. It's very simple. For everything that you put on the website, you put up text, a video, and downloadable audio.

TACTIC #38

BLOGS AND BLOGGING

Blog As Much As You Can And Stay Consistent

The goal for your blog should be four to five new posts a week. Don't be afraid. You don't have to write a book every time; three or four paragraphs are fine for each blog post. Consistency is important, so you shouldn't write four or five blog posts one week, take the next week off, and then write one the following week. You will lose readership. If you can do only three a week, then that's what you do, but be consistent and make sure that you post in a timely manner because once you start getting readership to your blog, they'll be expecting a new blog post around the same time of the week.

You should encourage people to subscribe to your blog. You should tell them sign up for blog posts and updates. You then send an e-mail blast to them when you do a new update, or they can subscribe to your RSS feed on your blog.

TACTIC #39

BLOGS AND BLOGGING

Create Multiple Content Pieces From One Blog Post

A great way to create multiple pieces of content from one blog posting is to record a video of the blog post content. Then you have the audio from the video stripped out and made into downloadable audio. Then you take that same audio and type it out or upload it to a transcription service. This way you can edit it. Now you have a video, an audio, and an article from one blog post.

The audio is easy because most of the better video editing suites have the ability to strip out the audio. For the article check the grammar and spellcheck it. Then you put it on your blog.

Now place the video on your YouTube channel and funnel it into your blog article. Now you have a V-log for your website.

Once you have a collection of articles, you can make a downloadable PDF or publish a book.

You can hire people to write or you can have guest writers. Ask your customers if they blog. You'd be shocked at how many people blog or know enough about something to write about it and would love the opportunity to write. Some of my clients ask their customers to write articles. You can also do that with staff members.

TACTIC #40

BLOGS AND BLOGGING

Blog Post Subjects Are Everywhere

You can get great blog content by answering your customer's questions, complaints, and concerns in a blog post. That's how you could easily get twenty a month, because if you're an active business, you're telling the whole staff, "Hey, whatever customer problem, concern, or accolade, I want to know about it." Write it down. At the end of the day, you pick which one you want to talk about. About twenty minutes later. Boom. Done. You've got one in the can. You're ready to rock.

To find more blog subjects, set up Google alerts, use key-word research tools, including Google's, to find out what people are currently looking for related to your industry. You will get alerts of the top things related to your industry. You could go to these websites and see what other people are talking about. If they're news articles, you can cite them, with permission, and use them in some of your blog articles. Don't copy and paste. That might get you into legal trouble.

You can find the most read books at the library. You can also find ideas for articles by going to bookstore websites and finding the most purchased books by subject. This will help you gain some information to help you decide what you're going to write about. You can also peruse some other popular news sites and blogs to see what they're saying, and use that as information to write your blog articles.

You could also do your own research by asking your clients, if you have a client base, what they would like more information about, then you can write articles based on that research. But it's

NOTES

always good to find out what the masses are looking for and reading about and what's trending; write about that, as long as it pertains to your industry.

DO NOT stray from your industry— no information about you personally or about other industries. Don't talk about competitors. None of that. Just write about what's hyper related to your industry. You decide whether you want to go highly technical if you are serving a technical market. However, it might be better to make all your content a little more palatable so that anyone could understand it.

TACTIC #41

BLOGS AND BLOGGING

A Quick List Of Ideas For Your Blog

1) Create a how-to video that shows the use of your products or services.

2) Blog case studies about your clients (with their permission) explaining the clients/customers problem and how you helped them solve it!

3) Find articles on the web or in print that you can paraphrase (not steal) and then elaborate and put your spin on them. Make sure you give the publication credit.

4) Solicit product uses from your customers and post unique ways to use the product.

5) Post about your charitable endeavors.

6) Post text and video testimonials.

7) Invite guest bloggers that write about your industry to post.

To sign up for free marketing information, or to contact me, visit my website at www.thomasforgione.com

NOTES

CHAPTER 17

Videos

Videos are a hot tactic in marketing today because with video you can tell a story using imagery and music to make it engaging.

TACTIC #42

VIDEOS

Make Video An Important Part Of Your Marketing Mix

Videos are a great way to promote your company and its products and services. A video could be used for testimonials, which in my opinion are much more compelling than written testimonials. You could use video for product demonstrations as well. Create a video of the owner of the company talking about how great the company is and how much they love their company and how it helps customers.

You can also record seminars on video,

and you can use videos from webinars and repackage this information and either sell it or give it away as content for people to download and to find out more information about your company and its products or services.

TACTIC #43

VIDEOS

Keep Your Costs Down

Video testimonials and off-the-cuff video should not be overly produced. Videos shouldn't look overproduced because true testimonials that look overproduced might not be believed. Smartphone-quality videos are fine for video testimonials as long as you can make out who these people are and what they're saying. Keep it short, under three minutes. If you are producing product demonstrations and intricate how-to videos, you should look into getting them professionally produced with proper lighting and crisp, clear audio. Or you could try it yourself; there are many affordable video cameras available that can record great video BUT make sure you have great lighting and sound.

Your backgrounds should be clean and nothing blinking. Some people will sit through an instructional video if its poor quality but not many will. Show yourself and your company in its best light. (No pun intended.)

TACTIC #44

VIDEOS

Use A Script For Your Videos

All video, except for testimonials, should have an outline and script of what you're going to talk about on the video so you're more comfortable. There are lots of websites that will instruct you on how to create a good video. Make sure that your personality comes through and you are genuine, honest, and likable in all the videos that you do.

Make sure you don't make sexual, political, racial, or religious comments. No Jokes. Don't go off topic; stay on topic. If you go off topic, your viewers will glaze over and they will stop paying attention because they get lost.

You can use your video in multiple places. Shoot one video then as I mentioned before, turn that video into a blog post. You can have it transcribed. You can have that video turned into a PowerPoint presentation. You can have that video transcribed into a report that you can sell or give away in exchange for an e-mail or mailing address. You could use that video as part of a compilation of videos that you'll give to your potential customers on a CD before they decide to do business with you.

You could post them on Facebook and YouTube, link them from Twitter, and put them on other social media platforms that you currently use. You should create a YouTube channel just for your business; every time you shoot a video, upload it.

You should encourage your staff to come up with unique ways to show your products through video. Make sure that your video is branded. Have your web address and captions on your video, put your logo behind you on a wall while

NOTES

you're speaking, or make sure that your video has a watermark in some places of your company name or what you do. There's nothing wrong with putting your company name and phone number on it.

If you have a problem with doing your own videos—maybe you're shy—there are a plethora of actors and actresses out there whom you can get to perform in your video, or maybe you have someone you employ who would be great on camera. Make sure they're photogenic and speak well. It doesn't have to be perfect; it just has to be done.

If you have a TV commercial you can use that video on YouTube, your blog, and Facebook to promote your company, provided you have the rights to use it. Video is very powerful. Think of the last time you went on YouTube to watch a video. Were you impressed? Did something in the back of your brain say, "Wow, I should do this for my company"? But you never get it done. The reason most people don't get it done is because they think it has to be perfect. It doesn't have to be perfect. After you do it a few times, guess what will happen? It will become better and better each time you do it, but if you don't do it once, you'll never see this. You'll never see it getting better. What if the first video you produce is not that great? Who cares? One person might think it's great, while another person might think you could have done a much better job. Who cares? If it gets the message across to the right prospect who then becomes your customer, you've done a good job.

To sign up for free marketing information, or to contact me, visit my website at www.thomasforgione.com

NOTES

CHAPTER 18

Webinars

Webinars are an effective method of training and educating your customers on the products and services that you sell.

TACTIC #45

WEBINARS

Webinars Should Educate And Be Convenient For Attendees

They can be at any time during the day but should be scheduled at the convenience of your customers. There are two types of webinars: live and prerecorded.

The beauty of the prerecorded webinar is that it works any time you want, multiple times, and you don't have to be there; just set it up and forget it. If your webinar is a very advanced training with specialized knowledge, you might want to consider charging for it. Especially if it has multiple sessions. You could charge anything from a small amount to hundreds of dollars to attend. If you are charging to participate, offer the attendees a video or a CD of the webinar afterward as a value-added item for an additional fee or free.

The best webinars that I've been on have a small number of attendees so when you ask a question it is actually answered, therefore you might want to limit the amount of attendees so you can handle the questions. If your webinar is longer than an hour, make sure you have great content in order to keep the participants' attention. Keep in mind that webinars longer than an hour are a big commitment, especially if they're live. Many people don't have more than an hour to watch a webinar.

Make sure that your webinar is very informative. You can have guest speakers on the webinar, to make it more interesting. If the guest speakers have an e-mail list, ask them to also help promote the webinar.

It's important to make sure you're using the right technology. The worse thing that can happen is that you start your webinar and your technology fails you. You need to be on a very fast server. You need to have great software to produce the webinar or to push the video if it's a pre-recorded video webinar. You need fast servers because you don't want lag time on the chat if you're having a live chat. That would be a disaster, especially if they are paying for it.

You don't want choppy video and make sure the audio is crisp and clear. If possible, the webinar should be monitored by a moderator that is employed by the webinar company. This way they can handle any technical issues. You want someone there who knows the technology and can put up images, sign-ups, and screens while you're teaching the webinar. If you get thirty or forty people on your webinar where you are selling something, you should be able to close some of those or get them to take the next step. A webinar is a nice, inexpensive way to accomplish sales goals.

TACTIC #46

WEBINARS

Use A Squeeze Page To Get People To Sign Up

A great way to get people to sign up for your webinar is the same way we've been talking about to get people to buy your goods and services: make sure they're qualified prospects through the use of a squeeze page. Create a great, informative webinar that will attract your prospects, drive them to the seminar squeeze page by promoting it through e-mail, pay per click, and multiple other media venues.

Use video and text that explains to visitors what they're going to learn on the webinar, why they shouldn't pass up this opportunity, and whether it's free or paid. Once they sign up they are placed on the webinar e-mail list so when it's getting close to the webinar time you can send out an e-mail, with a link and sign-in credentials, to remind them the webinar will be starting. That way they don't miss it or they're not late.

To sign up for free marketing information,
or to contact me, visit my website at
www.thomasforgione.com

CHAPTER 19

Print Advertising

Depending on the publication, print advertising can be expensive, so make sure that your customer demographic and psychographic is served. If you are not 100 percent certain that the market you're trying to attract is viewing the print publication that you want to advertise in, do not advertise in it. Never advertise anywhere by guessing that your customers and prospects are reading it. Always make sure that they are actually reading the publication before you advertise in it.

TACTIC #47

PRINT ADVERTISING

Print Ads Should Be Informative And Use Direct Response

Print ads should be informative and created in a way so your customers can respond immediately to the offer. They can respond by going to your website, by calling you, or by sending you an e-mail.

Placing ads in publications just for the sake of branding can be expensive and I don't recommend it unless you have lots of money to burn and don't care about tracking the effectiveness of the advertisement. If you need to use a lot of copy in the ad then do so. Less copy is NOT better than more copy as more copy usually outperforms using less. The copy should be written by a professional copywriter. It must extol the benefits of doing business with your company and buying your products or services. You can use coupons and offers in your ads or in print, but don't use too many. Too many will confuse, and you won't get any calls. Keep it simple: no more than three offers if you're using coupons, and that's pushing it.

Have a product image if you're selling a product or relevant image for a service and have beautiful imagery that attracts the readers eyeballs. Use pictures of people actually using the product if possible, and make sure the people in the image are within the demographic that you're serving.

NOTES

You need to place your print ad frequently. Placing an ad once and expecting results is gambling. Don't change the ad copy or images until you see that it is not performing as well as expected. Test the ad often to make sure that the ad is bringing in the desired results. If after the first run of the ad you do not see results, go back and change one thing on the ad. You cannot change multiple things because if you do you'll not know what worked, so you might want to change the headline. You might want to change an image. You might want to change the color of the call-to-action. You might want to change the position of the call-to-action, but you do not do more than one thing. The next time the ad runs, see if that increases your redemption. If it does, try to change one more thing to see if it will increase redemptions. If it does, you do it again.

Keep testing, and never be satisfied with your performance of your ad. Always be testing. Hire a marketing or advertising agency to create the ad, as many of the publications will give you a discount if you provide the ad. This is the best way to go. One of the problems I see when

NOTES

you let the publication create the ad is that they might employ only one graphic designer and eventually the ads all start to look the same and in addition, they might leave the copy or campaign strategy to the salesperson and if that happens you can be 99% sure your ad will be lost in a sea of blah.

Your ads must start with a strong descriptive headline. Never start your ad with a logo; start with a headline. Try to match the headline font to the same as the publication; use the biggest headline font and use the same headline style they use.

Make sure that your ad has strong call-to-action. If it's a large ad use multiple calls to action. Tell them what you want them to do. Make sure that your ad is in color. Color outperforms black-and-white. Try to be on the top right facing position of a page, not in the middle by the fold. Top right, back cover, inside back cover, front cover, inside front cover, and first page right inside front cover are all great positions to be in.

Ask for exclusivity on the page if possible. In other words, we don't want there to be two carpet cleaning companies on the same page or on facing pages. See if you could pay more to be the only carpet-cleaning company in the publication. Sometimes this is possible.

Print is not dead. If done right, it can add nice profits to your business.

To sign up for free marketing information, or to contact me, visit my website at www.thomasforgione.com

CHAPTER 20

TV And Radio

TV and Radio are effective ways to get your messages out to your customer profile. Keep in mind it can be expensive since you need frequency to ensure a successful campaign.

TACTIC #48

TV AND RADIO

TV Commercials

TV commercials are a great place to advertise your business; many local cable stations will give you many spots for little money. You'd be surprised. For example, we recently had a client who received TV commercials for as little as two or three dollars—sometimes a dollar spot—on certain cable TV stations. Remember, though, they still must be your target market. I've seen them as high as one hundred dollars a spot, but rarely are they that high for local cable. Just make sure that you're targeting your market.

As with all of your advertising your TV

commercials should consistently display a phone number and a web address. It shouldn't be cryptic. Try not to be cute or funny. Leave funny and cute for the companies who have the million-dollar marketing budgets. You need to get a message across in thirty seconds. If you can afford it, go for sixty seconds, but thirty seconds is all you normally have. Your commercial should be quick and to the point. Your phone number should be spoken in addition to being on a banner at the bottom or at the top, somewhere on the ad consistently.

You should also make sure that you tell viewers what you want them to do; even with the phone numbers at the bottom you should have a strong call to action such as, "Call now," "Call today," "Operators are standing by," or "Visit our website to place your order." You can be the talent in your commercial, or you can hire an actor or a semiprofessional or professional celebrity. If you can afford one, hire a spokesperson. But think it out carefully who you're going to use; make sure that they are the right market. People watching your TV commercials should be able to relate to the people in the TV commercial.

You can also use an actual on-camera, customer testimonial using the product or talking about the service in your commercial. Whatever you decide, TV commercials are a great, affordable way of communicating your message to the customers.

Once your commercial is produced, you can use that same commercial in different places, such as your own website, YouTube, and social media. Just make sure you get permission to use it in all those places. You want to get make sure it's royalty free, including any talent you used in the commercial.

TV commercials are just like any other form of marketing: they should be tested. To save some money, create it in a doughnut style. Doughnut style means that the TV commercial is the same at the beginning and at the end, but there's a middle that can be changed. The middle is usually reserved for when you change your offers, your calls-to-action, and so forth.

Again, test one thing at a time, so it might behoove you to get a few TV commercials shot at the beginning, which should be a lot less expensive than doing one at a time. So get a few different types with different scenarios and test them. Test frequently, and tweak them as needed.

TACTIC #49

TV AND RADIO

Radio

What goes for a TV commercial also goes for radio. If your market is there and listening to the radio station that you're advertising on and you're sure that they're listening, then it might be worth it. Remember to do your calculations before you make any media purchase. You need to make sure you know the number of people listening so you can estimate how many will redeem the offer and decide if you will make a return on investment.

Sometimes radio stations offer a barter scenario where you perform a service for them and they will give you the same value in radio spots. Many radio stations are open to this arrangement.

You also want to look into ten-second

spots. Ten-second spots are effective. Think about it: you can say the whole Pledge of Allegiance in ten seconds, so you can definitely get a short message across in ten seconds. Ten-second spots are usually much less costly than the full sixty-second spots.

The good thing about the ten-second spot is that once in a while you get lucky and it's ten seconds before the news or right after the news or right after the weather or the sports; those are the good spots.

There are also Internet radio stations that have a corresponding broadcast station, and there are companies that are just Internet radio stations. They usually do not have as many listeners, but sometimes you find some real winners out there. You should actively search for them to see what you can do. If you are promoting your website that sells products throughout the globe you could use Internet radio to promote in multiple markets.

To sign up for free marketing information, or to contact me, visit my website at www.thomasforgione.com

CHAPTER 21

Direct Mail

Many companies feel that direct mail is too expensive, but a carefully executed, strategic campaign can make the cash register ring, cha-ching! Don't send out thousands of run-of-the-mill letters or postcards before reading this.

Here are some tactics to get you started. Be creative and calculated.

TACTIC #50

DIRECT MAIL

Use A Highly Targeted List

Many companies use outdated means to acquire names and addresses. They guess (and usually are wrong) at their customer demographic and psychographic, and they buy thousands of names of people or companies who don't have the slightest need for, or care about, their product or service. Make sure you run a fresh customer demographic and psychographic profile of the top 20 percent of your clients who bring in 80 percent of your income. Then buy more of THE EXACT SAME customer profiles.

TACTIC #51

DIRECT MAIL

Have a Fantastic, Can't-Refuse Offer And Don't Let Your Ego Get In The Way

Companies send direct mail and other marketing communications that explain how great the company is, when the fact is NOBODY CARES ABOUT YOUR COMPANY—THEY ONLY CARE WHAT'S IN IT FOR THEM. The offer should be so great they cannot put the piece down. It should have them running for the phone with their credit cards. Think carefully about your offer. Have a few people you trust review it and see if it's as exciting as you think it is, then make sure your offer is customer-centric not company-centric. You should include company info, but that should not be the focus of the message.

TACTIC #52

DIRECT MAIL

Add A Guarantee

If you are mailing to a list of prospects who are not familiar with you or your company, take the risk out of trying your product or service by offering a "100% Money Back Guarantee" if they are not completely satisfied. Unless your product or service is of low quality, a small percentage of customers will take you up on the guarantee.

TACTIC #53

DIRECT MAIL

Copywriting

When writing a direct mail piece you MUST use copy that is designed to get the reader to act. There are many other things you should take into consideration, including personalization (with variable data), headlines, subheadings, image captions, post scripts, and calls to action. A professional copywriter should be sought out to ensure you are using great copy.

TACTIC #54

DIRECT MAIL

Use Multiple Calls To Action

Did you know that just by placing a strong call to action within the piece can increases calls? Examples of a call to action would be, "Call 732-555-1212 now and receive $20 off your purchase," or "You must hurry as this offer is only valid for the next three days! Don't miss this once in a lifetime opportunity!" or "Visit our website for a special offer just for you!" You get the idea. Put a call to action throughout the entire piece as some people will not read the entire message. You have to tell people what to do next.

NOTES

TACTIC #55

DIRECT MAIL

Use Creative Addressing

If you are using envelopes when sending direct mail, then I suggest you rethink how you will be addressing them. The goal of your envelope is to get it to the right person and to *get them to open it.* To get a better response, have your addresses handwritten. If possible, get your return address handwritten also. *When is the last time you threw a handwritten envelope in the trash without opening it?* I'll bet never. There are companies we use that will hand-address an envelope; some are local charitable organizations!

TACTIC #56

DIRECT MAIL

Testing the Campaign

If you are not getting responses then you need to change something. Test everything! Test the envelope, the offer, the headlines, and the copy. Let's say you have a list of ten thousand that you want to send your offer to. Create two pieces but on one of them change *one* thing. Send both to a thousand names. Then whatever piece gets the best response, send the rest out with the offer that pulled the best results. If you can afford it test more frequently, but *do not change more than one element at a time*. If you do, you will not know what worked.

TACTIC #57

DIRECT MAIL

Frequency Frequency Frequency

Many direct mail campaigns fail simply because of lack of frequency. One-shot marketing *rarely* works. When creating a direct mail campaign you *must* be in it for the long haul. You should mail at least four times a year to the *same* list. Research shows that advertising becomes effective after the third time. This is when awareness starts.

To sign up for free marketing information, or to contact me, visit my website at www.thomasforgione.com

CHAPTER 22

What's Next In Marketing?

In today's digital world there are companies, websites, and publications popping up every day that are after your advertising money. As a business owner you must be careful. Many shiny new marketing mediums will not apply to your business and will leave you with empty pockets. The best counsel I can give you is to always ask if anyone else in your industry is using them. If they are, get references from companies who are not competitors and call them to see how it's going. If they don't know if it's working, then it probably is not. If the salesperson cannot supply at least five to ten references with contact information, then I would pass, unless you are a wealthy gambler. Good luck and keep in touch!

To sign up for free marketing information,
or to contact me, visit my website at
www.thomasforgione.com